Mom

Dad

Brother

Sister

Grandpa

Grandma

Friends

Baby

Dog

Cat

Bird

Fish

Duck

Horse

Rabbit

Cow

Milk

Apple

Banana

Bread

Ice Cream

Cheese

Egg

Water

Head

Hand

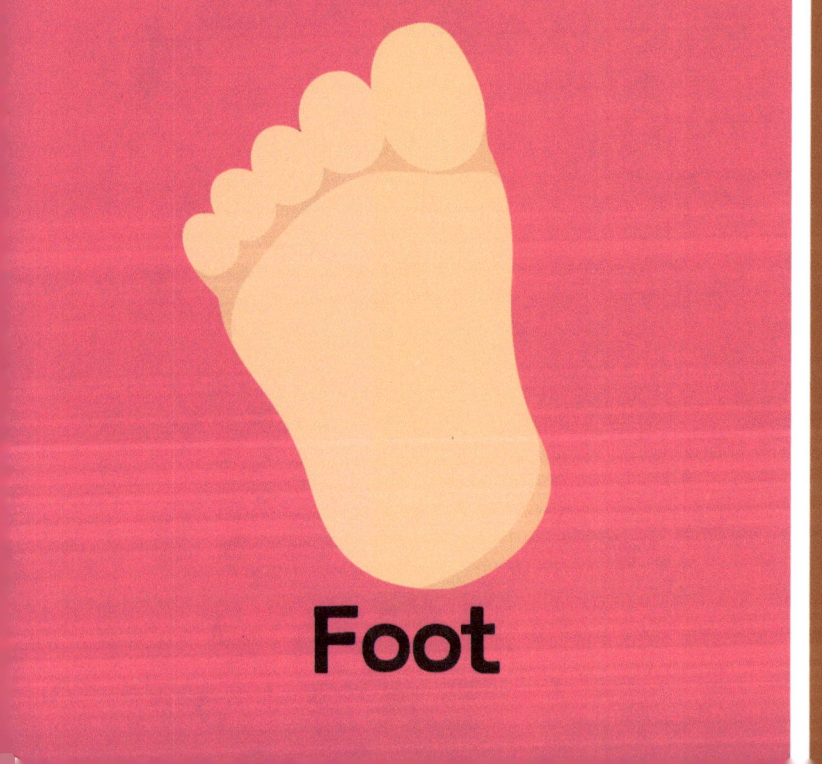

Foot

Nose

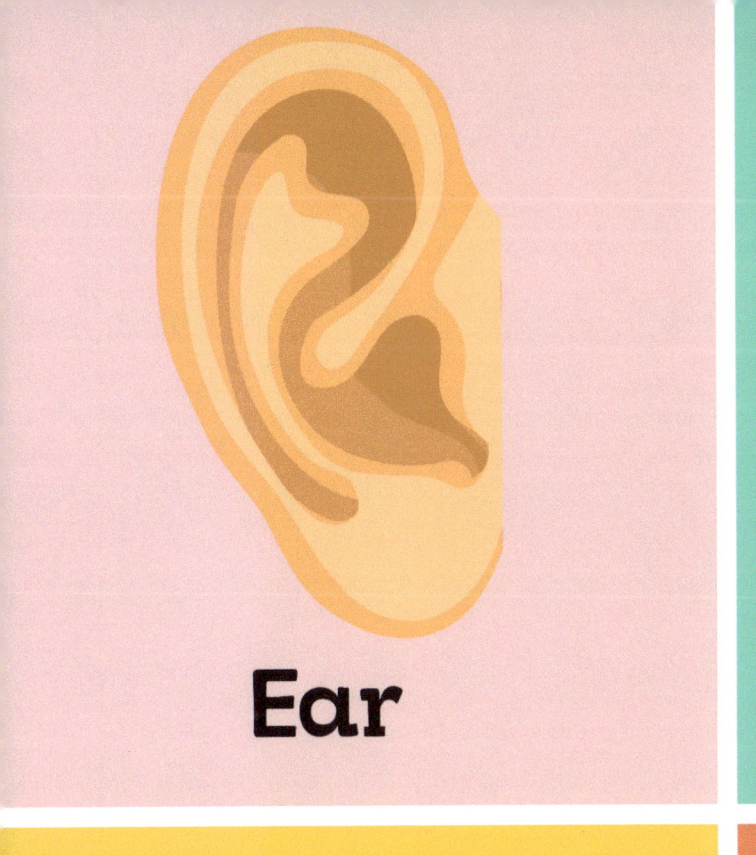

Ear

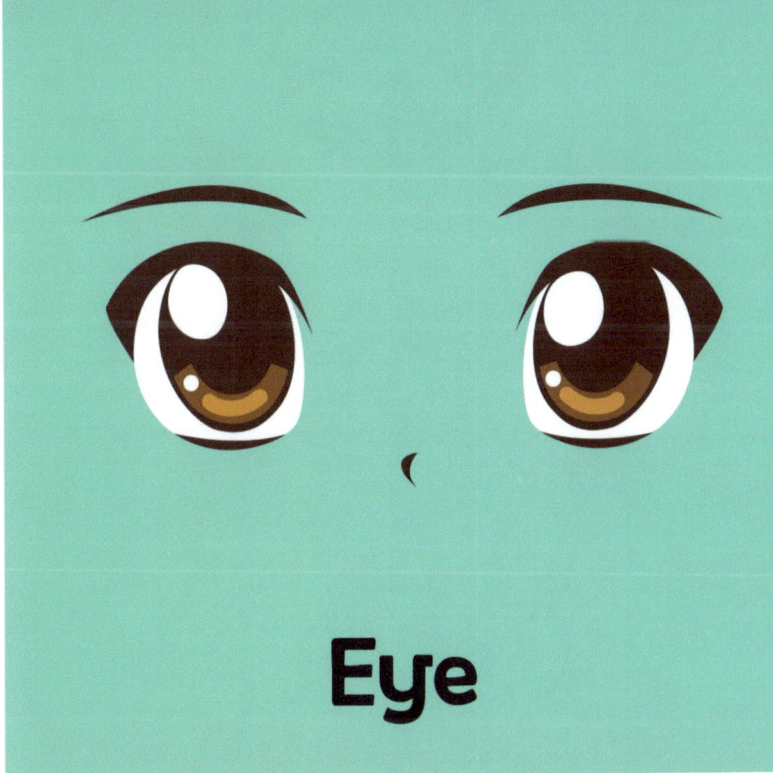

Eye

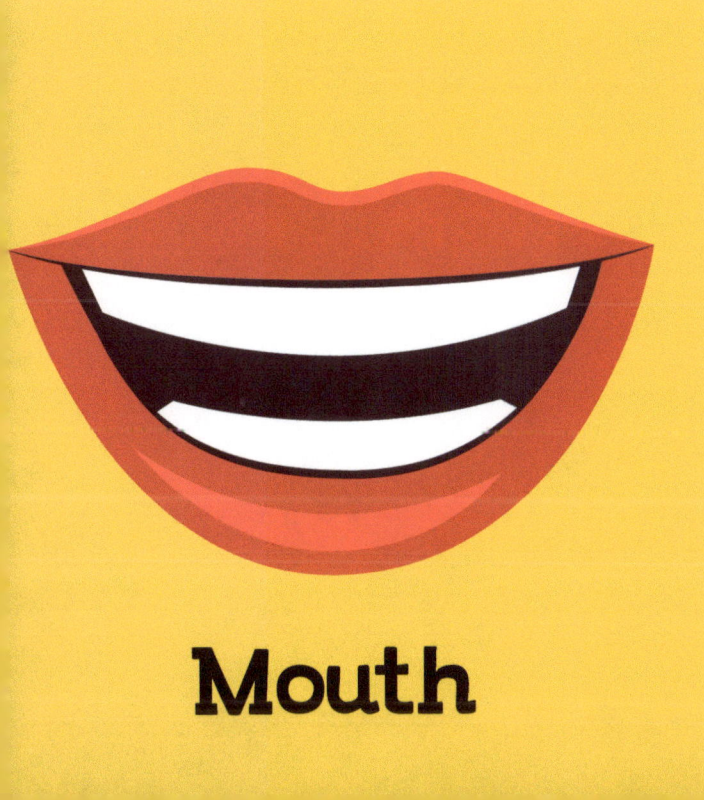

Mouth

Brow

Shirt

Pants

Sock

Shoe

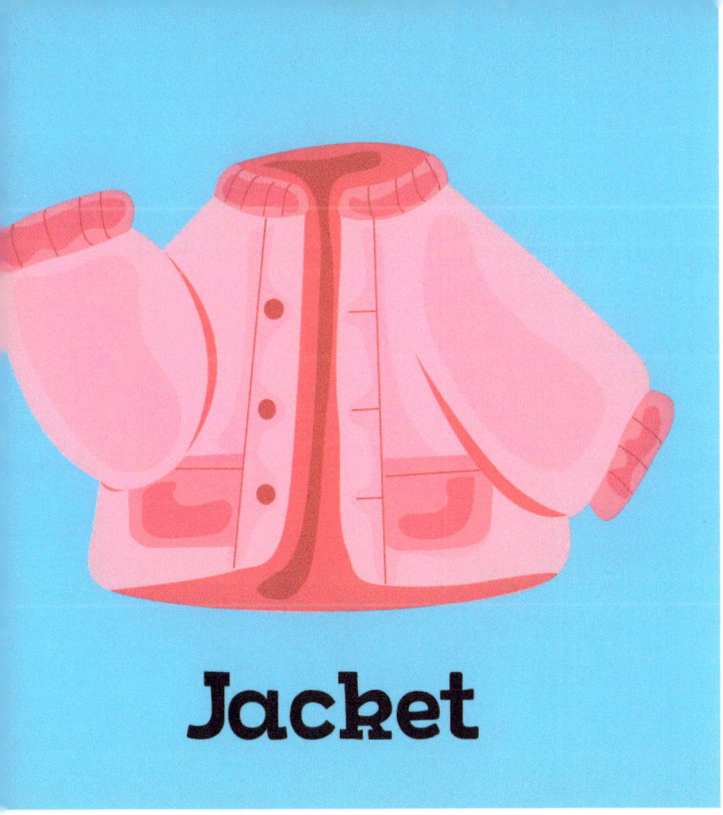

Jacket

Hat

Dress

Pajamas

Car

Bus

Train

Bike

Truck

Scooter

Boat

Airplane

Sun

Moon

Star

Cloud

Snow

Tree

Rainbow

Rain

Eat

Drink

Sleep

Walk

Run

Dance

Jump

Hug

Cup

Spoon

Plate

Table

Chair

Bed

Lamp

Book

Home

Park

School

Store

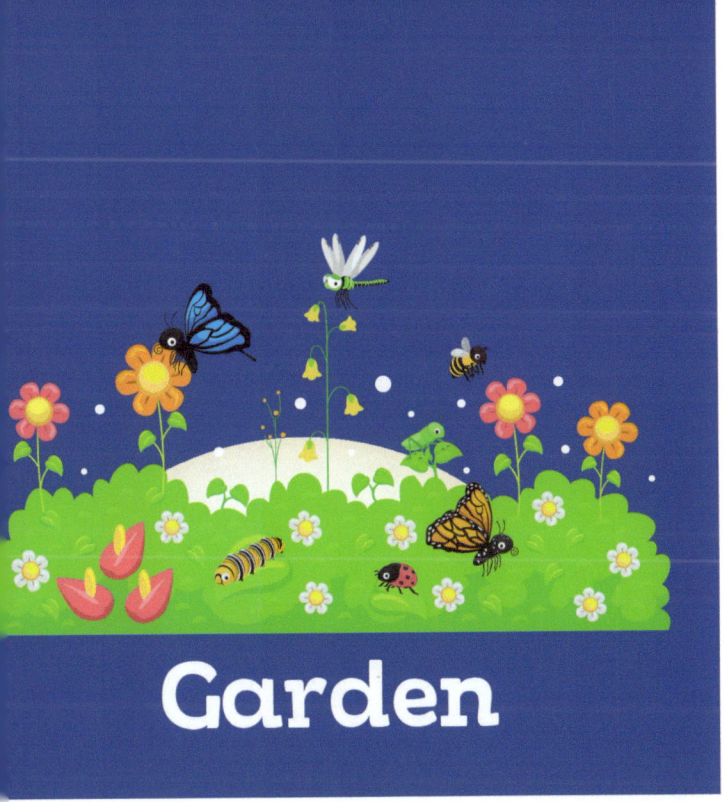

Garden

Playground

Zoo

Beach

Ball

Doll

Teddy

Blocks

Clock

Soap

Bag

Key

Happy

Sad

Angry

Scared

Surprised

Excited

Sleepy

Shy

www.ingramcontent.com/pod-product-compliance
Lightning Source LLC
Chambersburg PA
CBHW041449120626
46547CB00002B/393